WRESTLING

A PICTORIAL HISTORY

DAVID HOFSTEDE

ECW PRESS

A special thanks to Mike Chapman at the International Wrestling Institute and Museum, for providing some of the rare photos of professional wrestling's early days. Thanks also to Archive Photos, Mitch Brody, Brian Bukantis, Jack David, Corbis Images, the Everett Collection, Globe Photos, Kelly Kuhn, Howard Mandelbaum at Photofest, and Lisa Robertson.

NATIONAL LIBRARY OF CANADA CATALOGUING IN PUBLICATION DATA

Hofstede, David

Wrestling : a pictorial history

ISBN 1-55022-445-X

1. Wrestling — History. 2. Wrestling — History — Pictorial works. I. Title.

GV1195.H633 2001   796'.812   C00-933258-8

Cover and text design by Tania Craan
Cover photo courtesy of International Wrestling Institute and Museum

Printed by Transcontinental

Distributed in Canada by
General Distribution Services, 325 Humber College Blvd., Toronto, ON, M9W 7C3, Canada

Distributed in United States by
LPC GROUP, 1436 West Randolph Street, Chicago, Illinois, U.S.A. 60607

Distributed in Europe by
Turnaround Publisher Services, Unit 3, Olympia Trading Estate, Coburg Road, Wood Green, London N2Z 6TZ

Distributed in Australia by
Wakefield Press, 17 Rundle St., Kent Town, South Australia 5071

Published by ECW PRESS
2120 Queen Street East, Suite 200
Toronto, ON M4E 1E2
ecwpress.com

This book is set in Trajan, Futura and Minion.

PRINTED AND BOUND IN CANADA

The publication of *Wrestling: a pictorial history* has been generously supported by the Government of Canada through the Book Publishing Industry Development Program.

Canadä

WHERE HAVE YOU GONE, GEORGE HACKENSCHMIDT?

CONNECTING THE PAST AND PRESENT IN PROFESSIONAL WRESTLING

To say that wrestling is not like other professional sports is like saying that Karl Marx is different from the Marx Brothers. But beyond the obvious distinctions between the "sports-entertainment" exhibitions of wrestling and more legitimate athletic competitions, there is one other unique difference — the history of wrestling is not embraced by its current fans to the same extent that other fans acknowledge the heritage of their favorite sport.

Think about it — baseball lovers who root for Mark McGwire and Sammy Sosa are equally familiar with the names of Babe Ruth, Lou Gehrig, and Joe DiMaggio, even if they're too young to have ever seen them play. Football fanatics know about Jim Brown and Johnny Unitas, and basketball aficionados still debate the question of Wilt Chamberlain vs. Bill Russell.

But such is not the case with wrestling. Go to a live event now and ask the Rock's fans about Frank Gotch, or Joe Stecher, and the response will probably be "Who?" Guys in "Austin 3:16" t-shirts will cheer when Stone Cold Steve Austin fells an opponent with the "Lou Thesz Press," but they don't know Lou Thesz from Lou Ferrigno. And how many WCW fans realize that there was a "Nature Boy" before Ric Flair?

Sure, they may have tried watching vintage matches once, having stumbled upon it in a documentary or on ESPN Classic. And it may have been hard to suppress a yawn at the deliberately paced action, and the combatants who rarely (if ever) climb the ropes or hit the floor. Where's the music? The pyrotechnics? The catch phrases? The taped comedy segments between matches? They tuned in to watch wrestling and all they got was two wrestlers who were, well, wrestling.

You'd think the guys who would be most upset by this would be the stars of the golden age — Verne Gagne and Nick Bockwinkel and Bill Longson — whose contributions to the evolution of the sport have been forgotten by most of today's fans. Far from being offended at how little their achievements are now acknowledged, however, many of them actually encourage their disassociation from the current wrestling scene, which may be bigger and more successful, but is also (they assert) more frivolous and tasteless. "It used to be about who could beat who, then it was about who could outdraw who, then both," said Lou Thesz, "and now nothing matters but box office."

Well, with apologies to those fans who don't believe wrestling existed before Hulk Hogan, and those wrestlers who believe that wrestling ceased to exist *after* Hogan, I'd like to suggest that the more the sport changes, the more it really stays the same. Take a closer look at the in-ring styles, the personalities, the skills, and you'll find that the current superstars of the WWF and WCW have clearly learned their craft from previous generations, who performed in the NWA, AWA, USWA, and regional circuits across North America.

It is my hope that *Wrestling: A Pictorial History* will help to reforge the link between wrestling's past and its present. This is not a competition, a "my era is better than your era" debate, but a celebration of what has gone before, what's happening now, and what will surely be more exciting times to come.

CONTENTS

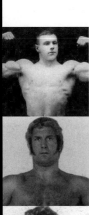

Born in 1878 in Humboldt, Iowa, Frank Gotch wrestled professionally in the years before and during World War I. Though he died in 1917, decades before the evolution of the sport into its current state, he is still renowned as the greatest wrestler who ever lived. Gotch defeated the most talented competitors of his era, including George Hackenschmidt and Tom Jenkins, with an aggressive attack that relied heavily on half-nelsons and toeholds. His speed was so astonishing that he once scored a fall on Stanislaus Zbyszko, a former world champion, in just 6.4 seconds.

THE
IMMORTALS

FRANK GOTCH

Still believed by many to be the greatest professional wrestler of all time, Frank Gotch wrestled over 400 official matches, and lost only six times. At the time of his death in 1917, Gotch was the best-known athlete in the United States.

F rank Gotch demonstrates the "two-on-one" arm lock, one of his favorite holds.

Gotch in 1911, the year of his second match against George Hackenschmidt. Gotch defeated the "Russian Lion" before a crowd of 28,000 in Chicago.

Burns
McIntosh
Sullivan
Gotch
Fitzsimmons Sharkey Harding
Jordan

No. 33

Dana
foto - S.F.

Gathered to watch boxing champion Jack Johnson in Reno, circa 1910, are: Frank Gotch (fourth from left), and boxers Tommy Burns (left), John L. Sullivan (third from left), Bob Fitzsimmons (right, next to Gotch), and Tom Sharkey (next to Fitzsimmons).

From the moment Ed "Strangler" Lewis agreed to job the Heavyweight title to Wayne Munn in 1925, no victory for a championship belt by any wrestler in any federation can be taken at face value. So, does this mean the titles are meaningless? Is a belt just another prop used by bookers to advance storylines and sell tickets? Don't tell that to the wrestlers, especially those who spent most of their careers with gold around their waists. To the old school champions — Lou Thesz, Verne Gagne, Ric Flair — the belt is an affirmation of skill and popularity. Wrestling's greatest champions all had exceptional ring prowess, distinctive fighting styles, and a devoted fan following.

THE
CHAMPIONS

Tony Folico, the national wrestling champion of Italy, battles middleweight and light heavyweight champion Charles Fischer. The match was filmed by MGM for a short subject feature on wrestling.

WILD RED"
BERRY

Prior to the evolution of a dozen separate wrestling federations, Wild Red Berry became America's undisputed light heavyweight champion nine times between 1937 and 1947. Many of his title matches were against arch-rival Danny McShain.

Three-time NCAA wrestling champion Danny Hodge wrestled his entire amateur career without ever being taken off his feet. He turned pro in 1960, and won the NWA junior heavyweight title six times in ten years. In 1957, Hodge became the first wrestler to appear on the cover of *Sports Illustrated*.

He never turned pro, but no book on the history of wrestling can be complete without mentioning Dan Gable, who may be the sport's greatest amateur star. Gable was the first American to win back-to-back world championships (1968–69), and the first to win an Olympic gold medal without ever having a point scored upon him.

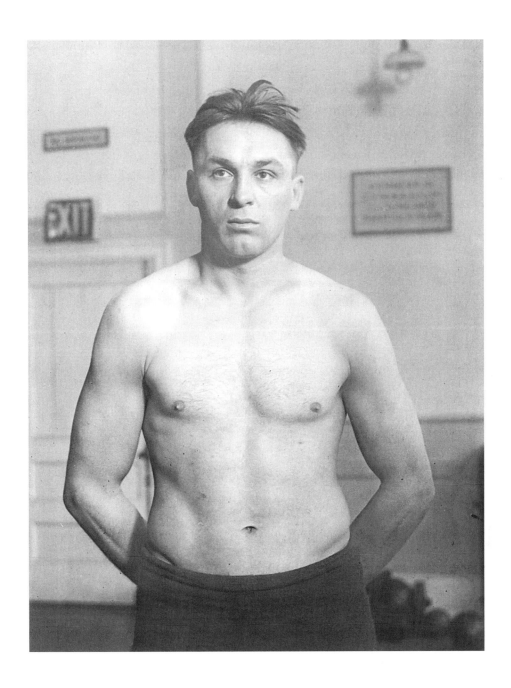

Joe Stecher became the most famous and feared professional wrestler after the retirement of Frank Gotch. A three-time undisputed world champion, Stecher was known as the "Scissors King" for his perfection of the bodyscissors hold. In 1916, he battled Ed "Strangler" Lewis in an epochal five-hour match, that ended in a draw.

Booooooo . . . just want to make these guys feel at home! It's the nature of the business for heels to become faces, and faces to turn heel. But some wrestlers will always be best-remembered as crowd-baiting, foreign object–carrying bums. Heels are skilled grapplers, even if they do their best work when the referee's back is turned. Fans love to hate them, and deep down, they know that it takes a truly great heel to make their heroes seem that much more heroic. It's hard to think of Verne Gagne without Nick Bockwinkel, Bobo Brazil without the Sheik, or Hulk Hogan without Rowdy Roddy Piper.

THE
HEELS

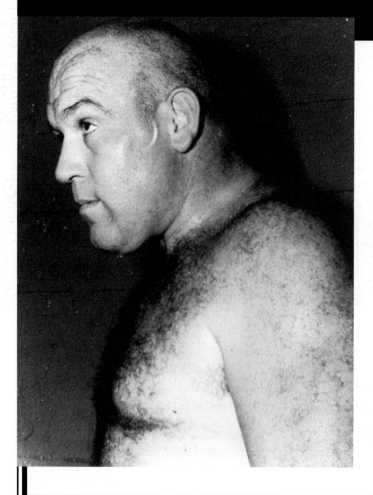

How much did fans hate Hardboiled Haggerty? He was stabbed in Minneapolis, shot in Louisville, and forced to jump from a second-story window in Duluth — into -18 degree temperatures — to avoid an angry mob.

Gus Sonnenberg was in the World title picture throughout
the early 1930s. Though his only title reign (1930) was
short-lived, Sonnenberg wrestled memorable matches
against such greats as Ed Don George and Ray Steele.

Dressed in a kilt, Scotsman Rowdy Roddy Piper was Hulk Hogan's arch nemesis, and one of the best microphone workers in the history of professional wrestling.

The Big Boss Man, a former Georgia prison guard, tried to bring law and order to wrestling. It didn't work.

Connecticut blueblood Hunter Hearst Helmsley reinvented himself as the arrogant, streetwise Triple H. Here, he applies his finishing hold, "the Pedigree," on the Rock.

Ox was named *Wrestling Training Illustrated*'s "Wrestler of the Month" in April 1977. This was the centerfold.

Most of wrestling's pioneers worked in the early days of the professional game, when they made their reputations with the introduction of a new hold or an original finishing maneuver. But the mantle of "pioneer" can also be applied to competitors of later eras, who broke through barriers of race or gender, often in the face of scorn from fans and fellow competitors.

THE
PIONEERS

Born in 1861, at the height of America's Civil War, Martin "Farmer" Burns was arguably the first nationally recognized professional wrestler. He won the heavyweight championship in 1895, and later trained the sport's greatest champion, Frank Gotch.

Ed "Strangler" Lewis is credited with the first "jobbing" of a heavyweight title in 1925. His intentional loss began the transformation of wrestling from sport to "sports-entertainment."

"Jumping" Joe Savoldi defeated Jim Londos for the heavyweight title in 1933, though Londos refused to acknowledge the loss. Such multiple claims to one world title were resolved with the creation of different wrestling federations, each with its own world champion, a tradition that continues today with the WWF, WCW, and ECW.

Jim Londos is credited with the invention of the Sleeper hold, one of wrestling's most oft-used submission maneuvers. During his 1934–35 NWA Heavyweight title reign, Londos successfully defended the belt more than 220 times.

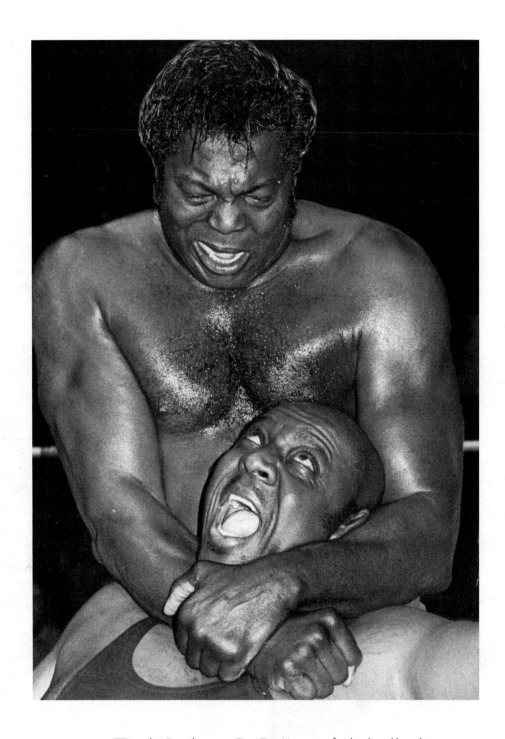

Bobo Brazil sets up Tiny Tim Hampton for his head-knocking coco-butt finisher. Brazil, the first black star to earn mainstream success, has been called the Jackie Robinson of wrestling. He was also a hero in Japan (where he defeated the great Shohei "Giant" Baba) and a title holder in the NWA, WWA, and WWWF.

C hyna, real name Joanie Laurer, trained with Killer Kowalski alongside Hunter Hearst Helmsley and, in 1999, became the first female Intercontinental champion in WWF history.

Dick Hutton invented the Cobra Twist, a back-wrenching submission hold, and developed the atomic drop as an offensive weapon. In 1957, his third year as a professional, Hutton replaced an ailing Whipper Watson in a match against Lou Thesz, and scored a shocking upset victory.

The first tag team wrestling match was staged in San Francisco in 1901. There is no truth to the rumor that Ric Flair was one of the competitors. The faster action and more complex strategies of tag team bouts quickly caught on with fans, and led to several variations. The "Texas Tornado" match allowed all four wrestlers into the ring at the same time; once these group brawls started, 3 on 3 and 4 on 4 matches were inevitable. The Mexican luchadores are masters of the tag team format — in a typical match, competitors fly in and out of the ring, usually over the top rope — at a frenzied pace.

THE
TAG TEAMS

The Brisco brothers, Jack and Jerry, were NWA tag champs three times in the 1970s. Jack Brisco (left) was a former NCAA champion, who also enjoyed a distinguished singles career. Jerry still makes appearances as one of Vince McMahon's "stooges" in the WWF.

The Becker Brothers, George and Bobby, were mainstays on the Mid-Atlantic circuit for two decades.

From Australia, Al Costello (center, upside down) and Roy Hefferman (dark trunks) wrestled as the Fabulous Kangaroos.

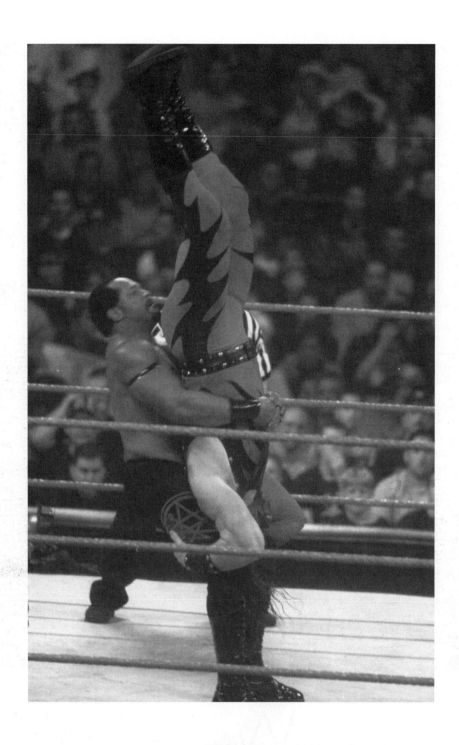

The Acolytes (Webster: "attendants on the ministers officiating at a sacred rite") seen here attending to Kane's rapid descent.

When Ivan Koloff and Superstar Graham were preparing to fight Parisi and Sammartino, Graham warned Sammartino that "we're gonna lay our full force square on your big nose. You're gonna hurt, you're gonna cry, you're gonna scream." (That's Lou Albano with his back to us.)

Victor Rivera posing with Dominic DeNucci wearing their WWWF World Tag Team Belts, having dethroned the Valiant Brothers.

For more than a century, the cowboy has been a positive, enduring symbol of American strength and independence. John Wayne and Clint Eastwood have inspired generations of boys to dream about riding the open range and defending frontier justice. So why is it that most of the wrestlers with a cowboy persona have turned out to be heels? Maybe they're a little grumpy being without their horse or away from the saloon, but that's no excuse for using lariats and branding irons as foreign objects. Black hats significantly outnumber white hats in the squared circle, and even the guys in white Stetsons, like Jeff Jarrett (Double J) can't always be trusted.

THE
COWBOYS

TOOTS MONDT
COLORADO COWBOY.

One of the first wrestlers to adopt a Western gimmick was Toots Mondt, who billed himself as the "Colorado Cowboy." Mondt later became one of wrestling's top promoters; in 1963, his secession (with Vince McMahon, Sr.) from the NWA's Northeast circuit resulted in the founding of the World Wrestling Federation.

Journeyman wrestler Cowboy Bob Orton appeared in the main event of the first WrestleMania (1984).

Terry Funk

Dick Murdock

Whether it's politically correct or not, American sports teams love to adopt Native American names, from the Washington Redskins to the Atlanta Braves. But only in wrestling do athletes actually dress the part as well. The heritage of Native Americans, with their colorful costumes and warrior reputations, proved irresistible to a variety of wrestlers, only some of whom (like Billy Two Rivers) can actually claim Indian ethnicity. Every federation had its Chiefs, such as Peter Maivia, Wahoo McDaniel, and Jay Strongbow, who wrestled as faces and brought honor to their Native garb. But some Indians, like the WWF's Tatanka, were not above a heel turn.

THE
INDIANS

Five-time NWA Heavyweight champion Wahoo McDaniel was a former football player for the New York Jets. His finishing hold was the Choctaw deathlock.

Chief Jay Strongbow goes on the warpath against Gorilla Monsoon. Few opponents could resist his "Indian deathlock" hold.

Indian Billy White Wolf, WWWF Tag Team Champion, with friend (not his tag team partner).

For years Luis Martinez wrestled under his own name, but now he wrestles as Apache Lou. "Most of my life I was ashamed of my Indian blood, but now I've read up on American and Mexican history. I'm proud of the way the Apaches fought and died for their rights."

No champion was responsible for more rewrites of the professional wrestling record books than Lou Thesz. In an era when dozens of regional federations crowned heavyweight champions, Thesz came the closest anyone could come (and may ever come again) to being America's undisputed wrestling champion. He won his first NWA title in 1937, and began merging territorial championships over the next 15 years. His 1952 victory over Baron Michele Leone for the California version of the NWA belt drew the first $100,000 gate in wrestling history. In the course of a long and storied career, Thesz, an unparalleled technical wrestler, held titles in five different decades. In 1990, at the age of 74, he wrestled a competitive match against 27-year-old Masa Chono.

THE
IMMORTALS

LOU THESZ

Lou Thesz was one of wrestling's most distinguished and deserving champions. In the 1940s, he returned a sense of dignity and class to a sport that had already sacrificed much of its legitimacy.

Thesz with his mentor,
former champion
Ed "Strangler" Lewis.

Lou Thesz sports one of the dozens of title belts he amassed in his 40-year career.

Women's wrestling first rose to prominence in the 1930s (a time when it was still illegal in some states) with the arrival of Mildred Burke, a technically proficient and photogenic champion who helped establish women's promotions across the United States. Burke and other pioneers, such as Elvira Snodgrass and the Fabulous Moolah, proved there was an audience for women in tights — title matches routinely drew crowds of 10,000 or more. Since the 1940s, women's wrestling has been a part of all the major federations, though its fortunes have fallen in recent decades. Recent champions, such as Sable and Debra McMichael, were more celebrated for their scanty ring costumes than their mat technique.

THE
LADIES

Mildred Burke ranked among the most popular women's champions of all time, and the first intergender champion, four decades before Andy Kaufman. Between 1935 and 1945, Burke offered $25 to any man within 20 pounds of her weight who could pin her. In 200 matches, she lost only once.

For nearly 20 years, between 1956 and 1984, the Fabulous Moolah reigned as World/WWF women's champion. She continued wrestling into her 70s.

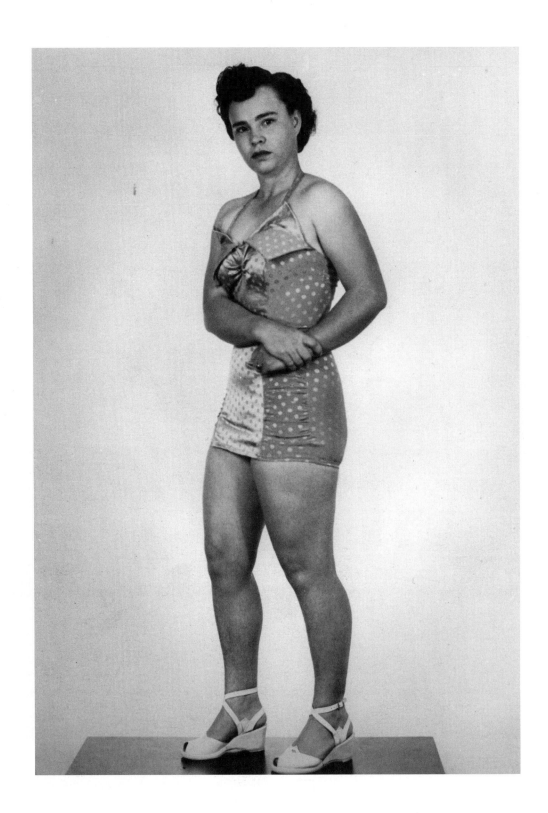

Jean Kennedy

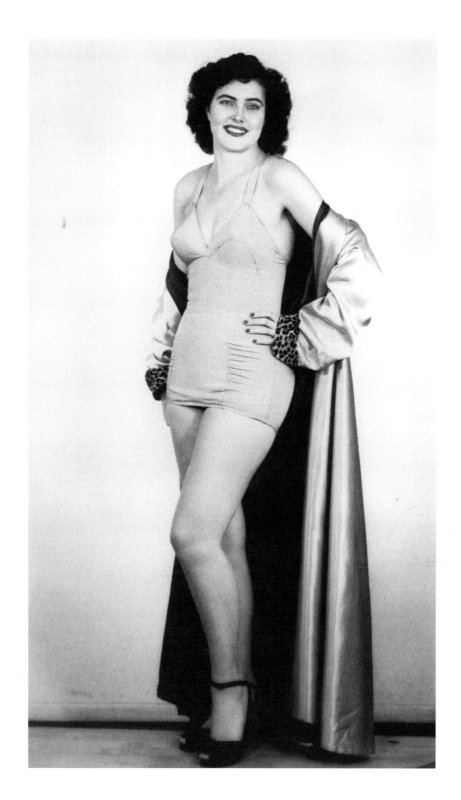

A nn Stanley

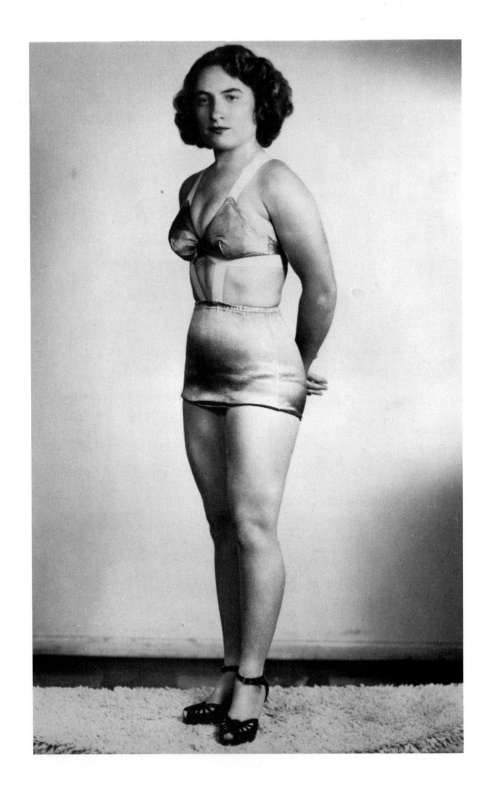

Ella Phillips

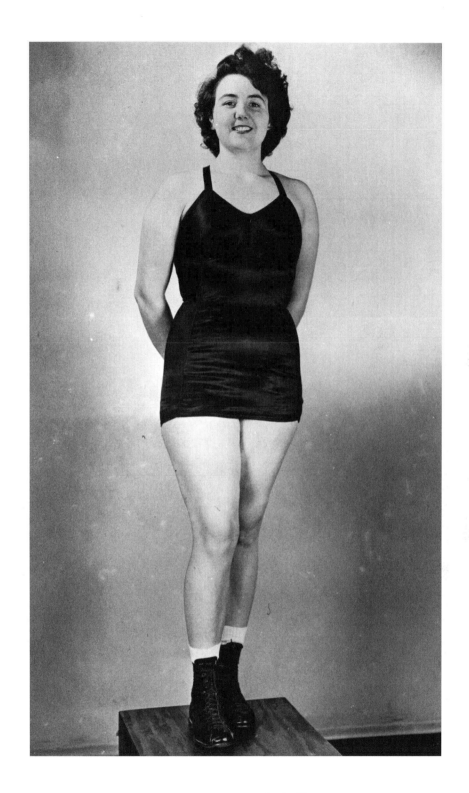

Lola Simpson

Before capturing the WWF Women's title, Ivory wrestled in the Gorgeous Ladies of Wrestling (GLOW) promotion as Tina Ferrari.

Once upon a time, every wrestler who laced up a pair of boots actually knew how to wrestle. Trained in the amateur style in college or the military, the first professional wrestlers brought a wealth of experience into the early federations. But somewhere along the way, that stopped being the case. Since the 1950s, scores of champions rose to prominence on brawling, showmanship, and an inexhaustible supply of dirty tricks. Though the evolution from sport to sports entertainment is now complete, there will always be a place in the game for a great mat technician, whether it's Verne Gagne in the '60s, Bob Backlund in the '70s, or Kurt Angle today.

THE
REAL DEALS

According to legend, John Pesek won the World Heavyweight Championship in the 1920s, but was so feared that no one would step in the ring with him; as a result, he was stripped for his failure to defend the belt. Pesek was a technical master, who debuted in 1914 and staged a comeback 40 years later. In 1954, at the age of 60, he wrestled seven pro matches and won six times.

Though he may be best remembered for his 1910 loss to Frank Gotch in just 6.4 seconds, Stanislaus Zbyszko (barefoot, pictured with 1924 Olympic wrestling champion Russel Vis) is worthy of a more distinguished legacy. A two-time world champion, Zbyszko was one of the most respected competitors in the early professional game.

At the dawn of the twentieth century, the undisputed American wrestling champion was Tom Jenkins. A powerful competitor who could also wrestle scientifically, Jenkins could claim victories over Farmer Burns and Frank Gotch.

B ret Hart, the "Excellence of Execution," fights off the crossface chicken wing hold of former WWF champ Bob Backlund at WrestleMania XI (1995).

Lazega

A collegiate and Olympic wrestler, Verne Gagne made his professional debut during the golden age of television wrestling. He held the AWA championship belt a record nine times.

Before joining the WWF, Kurt Angle won an Olympic gold medal for the U.S. as a freestyle wrestler in 1996.

The first wrestling superstar of the television era was a blond, slight-of-build, patrician-looking man named George Wagner, who billed himself as Gorgeous George. His flamboyant costumes and theatrical entrances are the source of much of what is commonplace in wrestling today. George walked to the ring, preceded by a male or female valet, who would sprinkle rose petals at his feet and spray perfume in the air. He tossed mirrors or golden bobby pins into the crowd, while insulting the fans who paid to see him. His escapades are still perceptible in such stars as Hunter Hearst Helmsley. Gorgeous George was a brilliant showman but he could also wrestle, and proved it by winning the AWA heavyweight championship in 1950. Sadly, his career did not survive after TV fans lost interest in the sport. George Wagner died of a heart attack in 1963, all but forgotten at the age of 48.

THE
IMMORTALS

GORGEOUS GEORGE

George makes certain the foreign object he slipped into his boot is ready for action.

nother precarious predica-
ment for George, courtesy
of Whipper Watson.

George, the flower child, in 1975.

G eorge apparently shopped at the same clothing stores as Liberace.

Despite his ruffly costumes and effeminate manner, Gorgeous George was actually a very talented wrestler, whose ring abilities earned accolades from such champions as Lou Thesz.

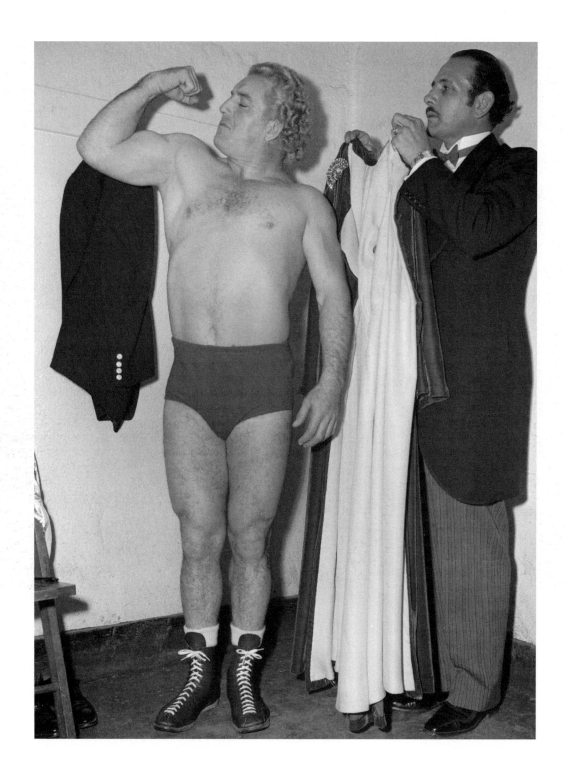

George, with his doting valet, prepares to make his entrance.

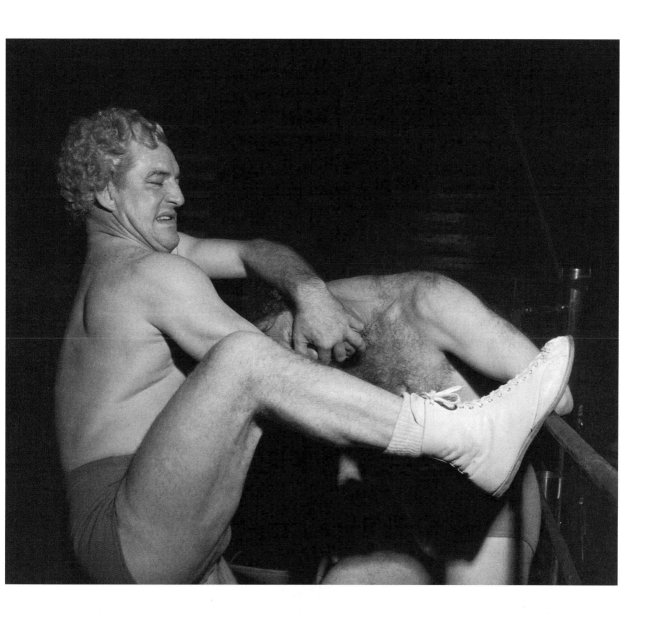

George frequently used the ropes in his offense, especially when the referee wasn't looking.

Wrestling experienced a rebirth in the 1950s thanks to television, a new entertainment medium then desperate for programming. Wrestling shows were cheap to produce, and audiences embraced them immediately — between 1949 and 1951, wrestling was broadcast six nights a week on four different networks. During the telecasts, the competitors were interviewed about their matches. During most of these amusing vignettes, wrestlers would brag about their prowess, and describe how they were going to dismantle their next opponent. These interviews revolutionized the sport, and hastened its evolution into sports-entertainment. Suddenly, what a wrestler could do "on the microphone," was as important as what he could do in the ring. It's no coincidence that Gorgeous George and Buddy Rogers were two of the most dominant wrestlers of the decade.

THE
LOUDMOUTHS

WWF President Vince McMahon became one of his company's greatest heels in 1997, after costing Bret Hart the championship belt at Survivor Series. He later began a celebrated feud with Stone Cold Steve Austin.

n his heyday, "Classy" Freddie Blassie inspired such hatred among wrestling fans that he often found his car vandalized after his matches.

"Superstar" Billy Graham had his hands full with Gorilla Monsoon. Graham's vicious attitude and dominance of the WWF in its pre-Hulk Hogan days inspired numerous wrestlers, including Jesse Ventura.

I f wrestling didn't pan out for Canadian Chris Jericho, he could have had a successful career in stand-up comedy.

Buddy Rogers, the original "Nature Boy," was one of the great arrogant talkers of wrestling's golden age. In 1961, after winning the NWA heavyweight title, Rogers grabbed the microphone and declared, "To a nicer guy, it couldn't happen."

If wrestling has made any positive contribution to the the upbringing of its many young fans, it's in demonstrating that heroes can come in all shapes, sizes, races, and creeds. Few wrestlers debut as faces — most win the support of the fans through skill and perseverence. Once their persona has been created, the heroes of wrestling are constantly tested through trials against the sport's nastiest heels. Sometimes they falter, and may even turn to the dark side for a time, but the setbacks are always temporary, and the best heroes never completely lose the affection of the crowd.

THE
HEROES

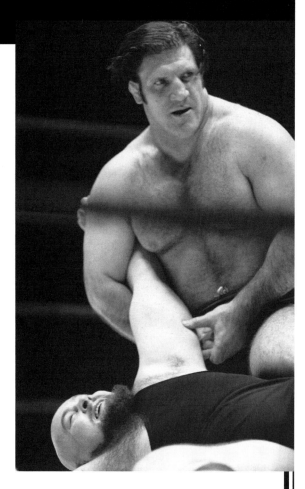

Burly Bruno Sammartino held the WWF Heavyweight title for an astonishing eight years.

The Ultimate Warrior's mad dashes to the ring and high-energy antics turned him into one of the WWF's most electrifying champions.

In the 1990s, Stone Cold Steve Austin became the most popular wrestler since Hulk Hogan. The "Texas Rattlesnake" began his WWF career as a heel, but he quickly won over fans with his no-nonsense style and profanity-laced tirades.

Charismatic Rocky Maivia, AKA The Rock, is the reigning king of the catch-phrase. A third-generation wrestler, the Rock has won the WWF title three times.

Earl Caddock

WRESTLER   IOWA

At just 190 pounds, Earl Caddock conceded weight to most champions of his era, but he defeated Joe Stecher for the world title in 1917. Caddock, acclaimed for his ability to break holds with remarkable tendon strength, walked away from his career to serve in World War I.

In the 1960s and '70s, nothing made a fan's heart beat faster than the magical phrase, "From parts unknown. . . ." Such introductions were reserved for masked competitors whose mysterious backgrounds enhanced their reputation for malice. Usually, it turned out to be a guy from Dayton, Ohio, or Sheboygan, Wisconsin, but what fun is that? The first masked wrestler appeared in 1873 on a card in Paris, billed as (what else?) The Masked Wrestler. Masks have been a part of wrestling ever since, particularly among the Mexican luchadores. The lucha libre style dates back to the formation of the Consejo Mundial de Lucha Libre (CMLL) in 1933. It's a fast-paced, exciting style that incorporates a variety of airborne maneuvers. The wearing of a mask was inspired by the elaborate masks worn by Aztec warriors.

THE
MASKED MEN

Mexican superstar Mil Mascaras was a three-time Americas champion, and the first masked wrestler to compete in Madison Square Garden.

The Assassin was one of the most successful masked wrestlers, and one of the best conditioned athletes anywhere.

"Number Two! Number Two! We Want Number Two!" This chant was heard whenever Mr. Wrestling II fought, having appropriated Tim Woods' Mr. Wrestling moniker.

W WF Championship Royal Rumble, New Haven Coliseum. Kane vs Prince Albert.

Holds and counterholds are all well and good, but why bother with a full nelson when a fist to the mouth will do? That was the philosophy of the brawlers; rough, tough, nasty characters whose offensive strategy seemed inspired by the Three Stooges — kicking, punching, eye gouging, whacking an opponent with a foreign object — no wonder these guys were usually heels. Most of the sport's best brawlers — Dick the Bruiser, Killer Kowalski, Mad Dog Vachon — knew how to wrestle, they just preferred to adopt a less scientific approach. Vachon, in fact, wrestled for Canada in the 1948 Olympics, and didn't bite his opponents once.

THE
BRAWLERS

Dick the Bruiser (right), one of wrestling's most fearsome brawlers, prepares to battle the 650-pound Haystacks Calhoun.

Wladek Kowalski earned his famous nickname "Killer" in 1954, after he severed the ear off Yukon Eric with a flying kneedrop. He wrestled competitively from 1947 to 1976.

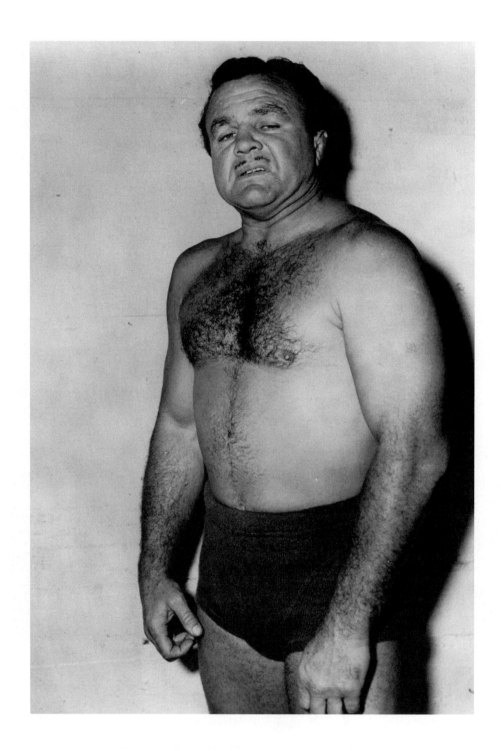

"Irish" Danny McShain was a bad-tempered, two-fisted fighter who competed in brass knuckles contests on the side, but he could also wrestle, as evidenced by his stunning victory over Verne Gagne for the NWA Junior Heavyweight title in 1951.

Donn Lewin was known as "The Executioner" for his aggressive ring tactics, especially against arch-rival Leo Garibaldi.

Patriotic fan favorite Hacksaw Jim Duggan spoke loudly, and carried a big stick — in this case, a 2 x 4.

As his fingers dig into Jack Brisco's chest and throat, Abdullah the Butcher's rage is so great that he tries to bite through the ropes. Does this man deserve a title match?

W restlers didn't come any meaner than the man known simply as The Crusher (here, inflicting punishment on Bobby Duncum). The Crusher, real name Reggie Lisowski, was a frequent tag team partner of another famous brawler, Dick the Bruiser.

The first acknowledged world champion of wrestling, George Hackenschmidt, was renowned for his outstanding build and remarkable conditioning. The "Russian Lion," as he was dubbed by the press, invoked gasps from arena crowds when he removed his robe to reveal a perfectly chiseled physique. Sixty years later, Dusty Rhodes could evoke the same response, but for different reasons. Hackenschmidt set the standard for wrestlers who looked as good as they performed, a legacy passed to such stars as British Bulldog Davey Boy Smith, and Lex Luger, billed as "the total package."

THE
BODYBUILDERS

The WCW (formerly NWA) heavyweight title traces its lineage back to May 5, 1904, when it was awarded to George Hackenschmidt after his defeat of Tom Jenkins. A champion at both Greco-Roman and catch-as-catch-can styles, Hackenschmidt was the most feared wrestler of his generation.

B asketball bad boy Dennis Rodman is subjected to the "torture rack" finisher of wrestler Lex Luger.

ungarian strongman Sandor Szabo defeated Bronko Nagurski for the NWA Heavyweight title in 1941.

Davey Boy Smith wrestled as one half of the British Bulldogs tag team, before taking the Bulldog name himself as a singles wrestler.

They rarely hold titles, they have ten defeats for every victory, and their t-shirts (if they even have any) don't sell well at the concession stand. "Jobbers," some might say, but no federation could exist without the steady, reliable role players who spend their careers filling up the midcard. It can be a thankless role, helping to get current and future stars over with the fans, but wrestling's journeymen are among the sport's most skilled performers, having to adapt to a variety of styles and taking a pounding at every house show, all for a fraction of their opponents' take home pay. So here's to the journeymen — you may have jobbed for most of your career, but it was a job well done.

THE
JOURNEYMEN

Having the best sideburns in wrestling, Canadian Hall of Famer Eric Froelich was a regular competitor for the NWA America's tag tream title, alongside Reuben Juarez.

Farmer Don Marlin brought a live pig to the ring for his matches.

The colorful career of Joe Malcewicz
began when he performed as "The
Mysterious Unknown" in a match against
the great Joe Stecher. Malcewicz, one of the
most talented and unheralded mat technicans
of the 1920s, can claim victories over both
Stecher and world champion Earl Caddock.

John Tolos, "The Golden Greek" — *Wrestling Training Illustrated*'s centerfold in September, 1976.

"To be general in Polish Army got be strong, eat much Kiebasy." And Ivan Putski's infamous move, the Polish Hammer, mesmerized many opponents.

Dan Hodge smushing an apple.

Viscera (on right, in case you didn't notice) and the Bossman at opening of the WWF restaurant.

The Zaharias brothers — all four could wrestle, but only George (left) left his mark on the sport. Billed as "the Crying Greek from Cripple Creek," George married Babe Didrickson, the world's greatest female athlete, in 1938.

Ray Steel

Ray Steele spent 15 years (some of them in the persona of "The Masked Marvel") in the NWA before finally earning a world title. He defeated Bronko Nagurski in 1940 for the world championship belt, and retired shortly thereafter.

They came from Germany, from Russia, from Iran, and from Japan — at least according to their official biographies. But many of the most fearsome foreign wrestling foes have little in common with their ring personas. Hans Schmidt, for instance, built a career as a Nazi-esque German heel in the decade after World War II, and could incite crowds to near-riots with his anti-American verbal assaults; in reality, however, he was a French-Canadian! Invader gimmicks are a bit passé, not to mention politically incorrect, in today's world of sports-entertainment, but for decades prior to our more enlightened era some of the greatest feuds in wrestling were created out of ethnic rivalries.

THE
INVADERS

Hassan Muhamed, the original "Terrible Turk," in 1928.

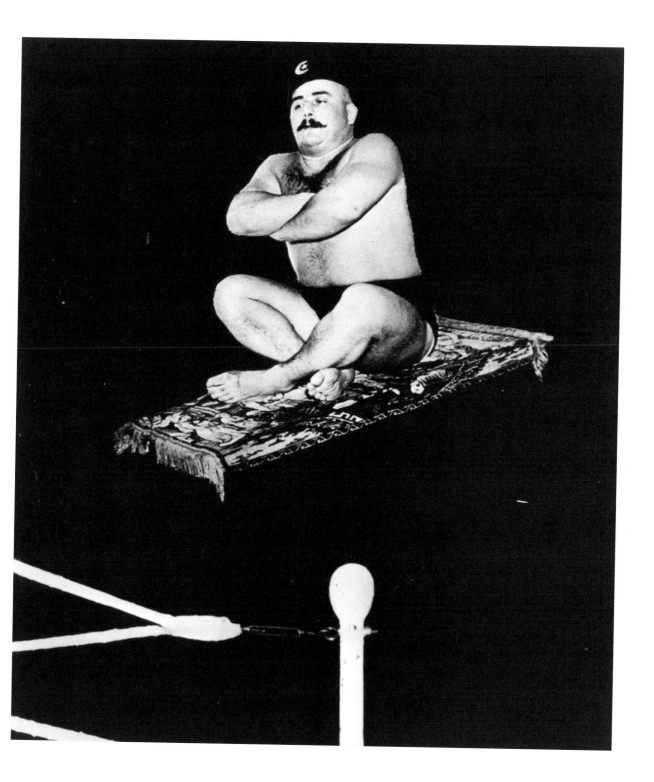

li Bey succeeded Hassan
Muhamed as the "Terrible
Turk" in the 1950s.

Proudly waving the flag of Iran, the Iron Sheik (right) inflamed the passions of American fans. The Sheik and his frequent tag partner, Russian heel Nikolai Volkoff (left), were managed by Freddie Blassie (center).

The goosestepping antics of Fritz Von Erich (being held aloft by Bruno Sammartino) infuriated Americans in the 1960s. Von Erich later renounced Germany and became a hero on the Texas circuit. Fritz is the father of five wrestling Von Erichs, including champions David and Kerry.

Kurt von Hess — North American Tag Champion.

Wrestling, like belching, is pretty much a guy thing. But there have always been female fans, especially at those events featuring wrestlers like "Heartbreak Kid" Shawn Michaels, who would bump and grind his way to the ring like a Chippendale's dancer, and "Bad guy" Razor Ramon, who ring announcers claimed was always "oozing machismo." With their *Tiger Beat* looks, flashy ring attire, and athletic prowess, the heartthrobs of the squared circle have brought wrestling to a wider audience.

THE
HEARTTHROBS

The "Heartbreak Kid," Shawn Michaels, held every major WWF title during his stellar career. His victory over Bret Hart in a 60-minute "Iron Man" match at WrestleMania XII (1996) was a throwback to the glory days of mat wrestling.

The matinee idol looks of Lucky Simunovich made him a popular draw, especially in the NWA's Hawaiian federation, where he won the Heavyweight title in 1952 and 1955. His most famous match was against the great Japanese grappler Rikidozan.

Dean Detton won the NWA Pacific Coast title eight times, and also held the federation's Hawaiian title, but his most famous title match was a defeat to the great Bronko Nagurski in 1937.

The WWF's man with the machismo, Latin heartthrob Razor Ramon. When Razor jumped to WCW, he reverted to his given name, Scott Hall.

T he ladies love Edge, who always makes his ring entrances through the crowd.

After television networks no longer relied on wrestling to fill their programming schedules, the popularity of the sport began to decline, and promoters scrambled to find new stars and new gimmicks to win back fans. Falling back on the old adage "bigger is better," they ushered in the era of the super-heavyweights. Gorilla Monsoon (420 pounds) and Haystacks Calhoun (650 pounds) were the most prominent performers in the weight class, until the arrival of a Frenchman named André René Rusinoff, better known as Andre the Giant. Mat wrestlers, whose entire offense focused on getting an opponent off his feet, were baffled at how to handle these titans, though such stars as Antonio Inoki and Bruno Sammartino developed impressive reputations as giant-killers.

THE
SUPERHEAVYWEIGHTS

Talk show host Mike Douglas gets a better view of the ocean, courtesy of Andre the Giant.

Man Mountain Dean had the weight advantage in almost every match he wrestled. Dubbed "the Hell's Kitchen Hillbilly" by writer Damon Runyon, the 317-pound Dean once wrestled 18 matches in one day, and won them all.

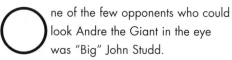 ne of the few opponents who could look Andre the Giant in the eye was "Big" John Studd.

When The Big Show debuted in WCW, he tried to pass himself off as the son of Andre the Giant.

Rikishi Phatu won many of his matches by grinding his large derrière in an opponent's face.

Like Laurel and Hardy, Sonny and Cher, and Mulder and Scully, some wrestlers are best remembered as part of a famous couple. Some are romances, some are rivalries, most wind up a little bit of both, but wrestling's supercouples have risen above temporary alliances and ever-changing storylines to carve out a permanent place in the history of sports-entertainment.

THE
COUPLES

Singer Cyndi Lauper teamed with Captain Lou Albano for a series of WWF appearances in the 1980s. Albano appeared as Cyndi's father in the video for "Girls Just Wanna Have Fun."

The "First Couple" of wrestling is inarguably Randy Savage and the lovely Miss Elizabeth.

I n one of the more outlandish recent WWF storylines, Triple H drugged and married his boss's daughter, Stephanie McMahon. Later, Stephanie betrayed her father and joined her husband's camp.

The people who ridicule professional wrestling tend to dismiss its competitors as clowns, not belonging in the same category as "real" athletes. How ironic, then, that those same athletes from other sports are among wrestling's biggest fans, and speak with admiration of the skill, strength, and training required to compete in the squared circle. Some have even stepped between the ropes themselves, either for a one-time match or as a second career. Football Hall of Famer Bronko Nagurski and heavyweight boxing champion Primo Carnera both switched to wrestling and held multiple titles. In recent years, Kevin Greene, Karl Malone, Dennis Rodman, Lawrence Taylor, and Reggie White have all faced the top stars of the WWF and WCW, with varying results.

THE
TWO SPORTSTARS

One of Britain's leading showjumpers, Harvey Smith (top), rides a different kind of beast during his wrestling match with Jack Mulligan.

H eavyweight boxing champion
Mike Tyson decks Shawn Michaels
at Wrestlemania XIV (1998).

Cincinnati Reds' legend Pete Rose's Wrestlemania run-ins with Kane, AKA "The Big Red Machine," have become a popular running gag among WWF fans.

Primo Carnera, a former heavyweight boxing champion of the world, switched to wrestling in 1941 and compiled a winning streak of 341 matches, before losing to Antonino Rocca in 1949.

B oxer Joe Louis, the incomparable "Brown Bomber," embarked upon a wrestling career in the 1950s, mostly to help pay off his tax debts to the government. Here, Louis tangles with Jim Bernard.

When Bronko Nagurski switched from football to wrestling, he brought many gridiron fans with him to the squared circle. Considered a novelty at first, Nagurski won respect in his new profession after defeating Lou Thesz for the NWA World Title in 1939.

Some gimmicks just can't be easily explained. Who could forget The Gorilla, a hirsute grappler who was wheeled to the ring in a cage? Or George "the Animal" Steele, who painted his tongue green and ate the stuffing out of the turnbuckles? Wrestling's oddities, whether fearsome, gruesome, or lovable, added flavor and variety to the traditional good vs. evil confrontations. Indeed, most of them began their careers as heels, as confused, hostile crowds didn't know what to make of them. Gradually, however, fans came to embrace these misfits, who seemed to appreciate the acceptance and applause more than their "normal" adversaries. There's a nice message in there somewhere.

THE
ODDITIES

Hardcore legend Mick Foley, in the bizarre persona of "Mankind," defeats Billy Gunn at Madison Square Garden. Foley often used one of his socks, dubbed "Mr. Socko," in a match by stuffing it down an opponent's throat.

From Death Valley, California, the Undertaker (right, with Paul Bearer) is a three-time WWF champion, and one of the most dynamic superstars of the past two decades.

The French Angel AKA Maurice Tillet terrorized opponents in the 1950s. Though short in stature, his powerful bear hug finisher caused many wrestlers to submit.

The Jungle Cat, Pampiro Firpo, aka the Eighth Wonder of the World, stated that "right now, Sheik, I weel hunt you down like a headhunter in search of prey! I weel lure you eento my own trap, my own secret strategy."

Look up "professional wrestler" in the dictionary, and you should see a picture of Ric Flair. He personifies the mental image of what most people envision when they hear the term "wrestler": the platinum blond hair, the sparkling, flowing ring robe, the braggadocio in interviews, and the complete disregard for rules and officials during a match. Through a career than spanned four decades, the Nature Boy stepped through the ropes with every superstar in the NWA, WCW, and WWF, from Dick the Bruiser and Buddy Rogers to Hulk Hogan and Bret Hart. He held world titles fifteen times, a record that may never be surpassed, and defended the belt in every corner of the world, from America to Europe to North Korea, where he headlined a wrestling card that drew more than 190,000 fans.

THE
IMMORTALS

RIC FLAIR

Ric Flair jumped to the WWF in 1991, and captured that federation's title in 1992.

With his silver white hair and gaudy ring robes, "Nature Boy" Ric Flair personified professional wrestling for two generations of fans.

"There's no bigger kick in the world," says Ric Flair, "than to see a guy lying in pain on the canvas. Ever watch a guy clutching a limb which he takes is broken? Show me a foe with a broken arm and I'll show you a happy Ric Flair!"

Randy Gordon, author of "Top Secret" from *Inside Wrestling*, tells this story: Someone left trick chewing gum in Ric's dressing room; the "Nature Boy" chewed and chewed so vigorously that he pulled some muscles in his jaw.

"It was a pleasure to see him that night," said Gordon, "with his mouth shut."

Nothing is more satisfying to a wrestling fan than the first match between two champions, a once-in-a-lifetime special event, or the culmination of a long-simmering feud. Some of wrestling's greatest matches have been wrestling clinics, others have looked more like circus sideshows. But to the fans who saw them live, they're a memory to treasure.

THE
GREAT MATCHES

Frank Gotch wrestles George Hackenschmidt in Chicago's Comiskey Park, in 1911. Gotch scored his second victory over the Russian Lion in what was then the most eagerly anticipated rematch in the sport's history.

Stanislaus Zbyszko (left) prepares to wrestling Ed "Strangler" Lewis on May 6, 1921. In what was viewed as a comeback match for the great Polish champion, Zbyszko defeated Lewis for the title.

The Ultimate Warrior's arm is raised in victory by opponent Hulk Hogan, after their exciting main event melée at Wrestlemania VI (1990).

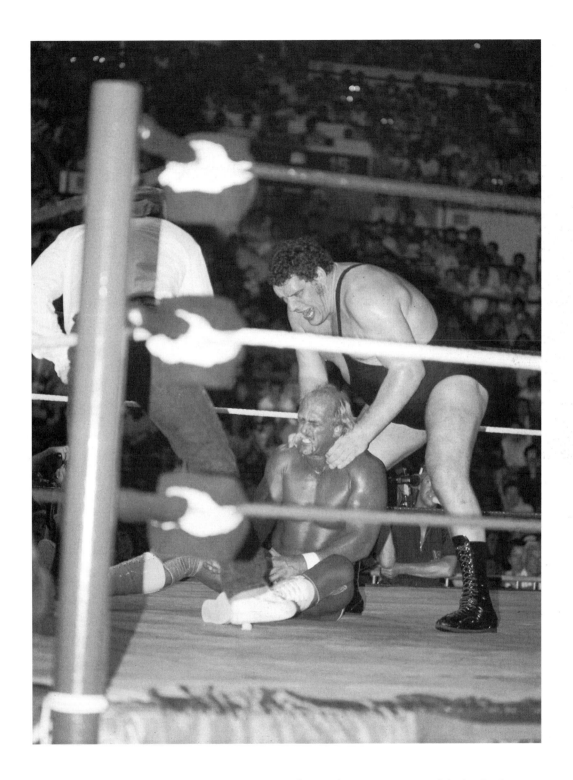

The war between Hogan and Andre the Giant culminated at WrestleMania III (1987), where Hogan won the WWF title before 90,000 fans.

Tag team matches in the modern era don't get any better than the Dudley Boys vs. the Hardy Boyz.

n 1976, Muhammad Ali and Japanese wrestling great Antonio Inoki battled to a 15-round draw in Tokyo.

I n one of the most famous boxer-wrestler matches, Andre the Giant and boxer Chuck Wepner fought a tag team match against Muhammad Ali and wrestler Stan Hansen (right, with Andre). The match took place in New York's Shea Stadium, before 32,000 fans.

Clothes don't necessarily make the wrestler, but some of the sport's most unforgettable fashion plates certainly created a style all their own, and as a result their ring entrances are as memorable now than anything they did after the bell rang. A plain old ring robe was transformed into a glittering, multi-colored dreamcoat when draped over such competitors as Gorgeous George, Classy Freddie Blassie, and Nature Boy Ric Flair. Capes became a popular accessory with guys like Randy Savage and Jushin Liger. Jesse "the Body" Ventura often wrapped himself in feathered boas, but the citizens of Minnesota elected him governor anyway.

THE
FANCY DRESSERS

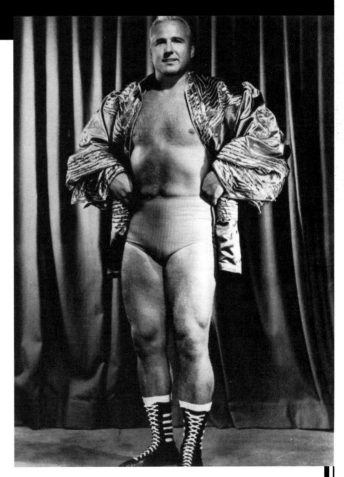

Dr. Jerry Graham, along with his brother Eddie, won the WWF tag titles three times in the 1950s.

outh American Raul Mota was a bit too burly for the lucha libre style, but he won the NWA Americas tag title with David Morgan in 1975.

Ladies and gentlemen, the governor of the great state of Minnesota: Jesse "the Body" Ventura in his WWF days.

Flashy, multicolored capes, cowboy hats, and sunglasses were the trademarks of Randy "Macho Man" Savage.

Ted DiBiase, the "Million Dollar Man," couldn't win the WWF title belt, so he bought a belt of his own.

The history of professional wrestling can be divided into two chapters: before Hulk Hogan, and after. Old school fans will protest that the sport lost something at the dawn of Hulkamania, and they're right, but it gained a great deal more. Hogan brought wrestling back into the mainstream, on the strength of his larger-than-life personality and charisma. He returned wrestling to primetime network television, and turned title matches back into actual events. He was the champion when the era of "sports entertainment" began, and he personified that term for a generation of fans. Could Hogan do a senton bomb? A frankensteiner? A missile drop kick? Never. But why bother when he can bring an audience to its feet with a simple leg drop? His technical skills are beside the point, because wrestling didn't make Hulk Hogan — Hulk Hogan made wrestling.

THE
IMMORTALS

HULK HOGAN

Fans loved Sergeant Slaughter (left), wrestling's answer to G.I. Joe, until he sold out his country and teamed with the Iron Sheik. That's when Hulk Hogan busted the Sarge back to Private at WrestleMania VII (1991).

ifferent company, same winning ways: Hogan joined WCW in 1994 and defeated Ric Flair for the World Title.

Hulk Hogan (right) and Rowdy Roddy
Piper personified good and evil in
the World Wrestling Federation.

Hogan drops a mighty elbow on Don Muraco.

Chatting with *Tonight Show* guest-host Joan Rivers.

Hogan defeated former sumo wrestler Yokozuna at WrestleMania IX (1994). It was his last significant match in the World Wrestling Federation.

When Hogan joined Scott Hall and Kevin Nash in the New World Order, it was the most shocking heel turn in wrestling history.

Mat wrestling, which evolved out of the Greco-Roman and catch-as-catch-can styles of the amateur game, dominated the professional ranks until the 1950s, when an exciting new breed of wrestlers added an aerial assault to their ground game. Edouard Carpentier, a former high wire star in a European circus, was among the first to fly above the ropes. He used his acrobatic training to thrill fans with such then-revolutionary moves as his back somersault finisher. Soccer player Antonino Rocca popularized the dropkick, and the first lucha libre stars used their speed and agility as their primary offensive weapon. The tradition of the great high fliers lives on today in the Hardy Boys and Rey Misterio, Jr.

THE
HIGH FLIERS

French star Jean Dubois plants a drop kick on opponent Jack Evans during a WWWF match in 1971.

Antonino Rocca, a former soccer player, rarely used his arms in the ring — he didn't need them. One of the most popular wrestlers of the 1950s, Rocca ended Primo Carnera's 341-match winning streak with his devastating dropkick.

The Canadian Stomper smashes Harley Race's head in a revenge match. Says the Stomper: "I want to rearrange his puss the most painful way possible."

inoki coming in on a top corner buckle flying body press on a McGuire twin.

The most famous women in wrestling are not grapplers like Mildred Burke or the Fabulous Moolah, but the beautiful, bodyful managers, girlfriends, and valets who accompany male stars to the ring. The job consists solely of wearing sexy outfits, and distracting referees and opponents to influence the outcome of a match. Though Moolah, as Lillian Ellison, began her career back in 1956 as the fetching "Slave Girl" to a wrestler billed as Elephant Boy, the addition of glamor girls is really a modern phenomenon, that took off in the mid-80s with the debuts of Missy Hyatt in the UWF, and the lovely Miss Elizabeth, who became as big a star in the WWF as her husband, Macho Man Randy Savage.

THE
GLAMOR GIRLS

When the demure Miss Elizabeth removed her skirt at 1988's SummerSlam, everybody forgot who was in the ring.

Sexy Terri Runnels, flanked by the Hardy Boyz, was affectionately known as the "She-devil."

One of the great names in wrestling, Gorgeous George, was revived by Randy Savage's girlfriend. This George couldn't wrestle, but no one seemed to mind.

Rena Mero became the WWF's premier glamour girl in 1998, and her nude pictorial in *Playboy* generated the highest sales in the magazine's history.

M ildred Burke was the first universally acclaimed woman's wrestling champion.

PHOTO CREDITS